Steven Spielberg

A Little Golden Book® Biography

By Geof Smith
Illustrated by Luke Flowers

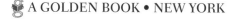 A GOLDEN BOOK • NEW YORK

Text copyright © 2024 by Geof Smith
Cover art and interior illustrations copyright © 2024 by Luke Flowers
All rights reserved. Published in the United States by Golden Books, an imprint of
Random House Children's Books, a division of Penguin Random House LLC, 1745 Broadway,
New York, NY 10019. Golden Books, A Golden Book, A Little Golden Book, the G colophon,
and the distinctive gold spine are registered trademarks of Penguin Random House LLC.
rhcbooks.com
Educators and librarians, for a variety of teaching tools, visit us at RHTeachersLibrarians.com
Library of Congress Control Number: 2023951549
ISBN 978-0-593-71007-4 (trade) — ISBN 978-0-593-71008-1 (ebook)
Printed in the United States of America
10 9 8 7 6 5 4 3 2 1

Steven Allan Spielberg was born on December 18, 1946, in Cincinnati, Ohio. He has three younger sisters, Anne, Sue, and Nancy. His mother, Leah, was a talented piano player. His father, Arnold, was an electrical engineer who worked on some of the first computers.

Steven was a shy child who liked to spend time with his family. They made him feel loved and safe.

The Spielbergs moved to New Jersey in 1952. One night, Steven's father took him to see his first movie, *The Greatest Show on Earth*. His favorite scene showed a train crash. It was so exciting—and a little scary.

His father explained that the crash wasn't real. Six-year-old Steven was confused. How could something be fake *and* so thrilling?

Back home, Steven liked acting out the train crash with his toys. However, his father quickly grew tired of having to fix the broken trains. This gave Steven an idea: he recreated the crash one more time but filmed it with the family movie camera. Now he could watch the scene over and over.

From then on, Steven fell in love with movies—watching *and* making them!

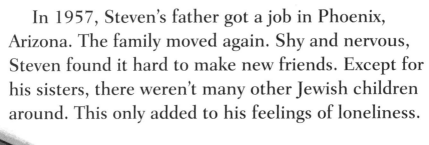

In 1957, Steven's father got a job in Phoenix, Arizona. The family moved again. Shy and nervous, Steven found it hard to make new friends. Except for his sisters, there weren't many other Jewish children around. This only added to his feelings of loneliness.

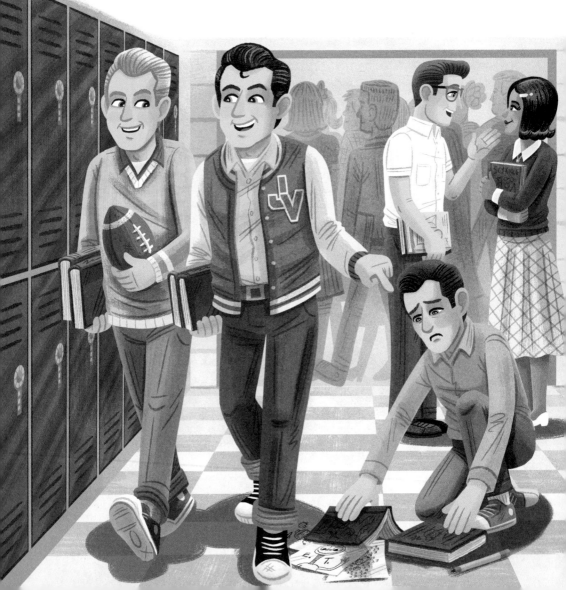

Making movies helped Steven meet people and feel more confident. He liked being a director. He knew how to work the camera and get the best shots. He could tell his actors what to do.

Steven filmed family camping trips and made monster movies with his sisters. He also made a Western with his Boy Scout troop and earned a merit badge.

While still in high school, Steven made a science fiction film called *Firelight*. It was over two hours long and was shown at a local theater. Steven arrived at the premiere in a rented limousine!

Firelight was a true family project. His father helped build sets. His sisters acted in the movie and worked behind the scenes. His mother hung the letters on the theater marquee.

The very next day, the Spielbergs moved to California. Life in their new home wasn't a happy one. Steven's parents soon separated. He stayed with his father. His mother and sisters returned to Arizona. Steven was sad. He missed having his whole family around him.

PHOENIX
LITTLE THEATRE
PREMIERE MOVIE
FIRELIGHT
MARCH 24   8 PM
FEATURE PRESENTATION

After high school, all Steven wanted to do was direct films. His father wanted him to go to college.

He started college in 1965, but a short film he made called *Amblin'* caught the attention of Universal Studios. Steven dropped out of school and began working in Hollywood.

At just twenty-one years old, Steven became the youngest person hired as a director by a major studio. He directed spooky stories, mysteries, and dramas for television. People were amazed that someone so young had so much talent.

Before long, Steven was preparing to bring *Jaws*, a bestselling book about a giant shark, to the big screen. He wanted it to be fun and scary, like the monster movies he loved as a boy. But filming at sea was difficult. And the star of the movie, a mechanical shark that Steven called Bruce, broke down a lot.

Steven worried the movie would be a failure and his film career would be over.

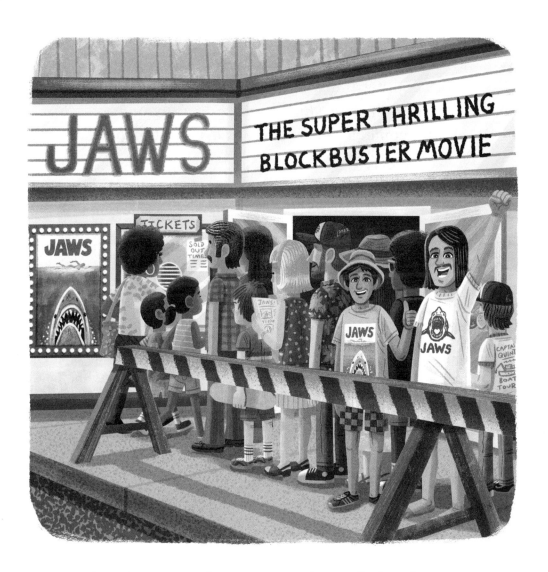

But *Jaws* was a huge success! People lined up
to see it again and again. It is considered the first
summer blockbuster, a wildly popular movie that
makes a lot of money.

At twenty-eight years old, Steven was suddenly
famous!

Over the next few years, Steven made many more popular films. He wrote and directed *Close Encounters of the Third Kind*, a dazzling movie about people contacting aliens from outer space.

In 1981, he teamed up with his friend George Lucas, the director of *Star Wars*. Together, they made *Raiders of the Lost Ark*, which followed the adventures of a daring archaeologist named Indiana Jones.

The following year, Steven directed a movie called *E.T. the Extra-Terrestrial*. It was the story of a boy named Elliott who finds and protects a lost alien. The film became one of the most successful and best-loved movies of all time.

Even though it was a fantastic adventure, *E.T.* was a very personal movie for Steven. He put a lot of his childhood into the story. Like Steven, Elliott was a lonely boy whose parents were separated.

Steven was known for using the newest special effects in his movies. When he made *Jurassic Park,* he wanted the dinosaurs to be as realistic as possible. He understood that computer-generated images, or CGI, would make awesome dinosaurs.

Audiences were amazed, and the way movies were made was changed forever!

   Audiences loved Steven's work, but some critics
said he only made fun movies for kids. And then, in
1993, he directed *Schindler's List*.

   It was a very serious and sad film about a man
who helped Jewish people during World War II.
Many people thought it was Steven's best movie yet.

Because it was such an important story, Steven didn't feel right being paid for the work. Instead, he used the money he earned from *Schindler's List* to start the USC Shoah Foundation. *Shoah* is the Hebrew word for *catastrophe*. This group records the stories of people hurt by wars so that they'll never be forgotten.

Something else happened because of *Schindler's
List*—Steven finally won his first Academy Award for
Best Director. It was a prize he had wanted for a long
time. His mother was in the audience, and she was
very proud.

He made his parents happy again by going back
to school and graduating from college in 2002. He
submitted *Schindler's List* as a class project.

Over the years, Steven made many more films. He cofounded a production company, Amblin Entertainment, and a movie studio, DreamWorks Pictures.

He likes helping young filmmakers get started in the business. And he enjoys working with old friends. The same composer, writers, actors, camera people, and editor have worked with him again and again. It's like Steven has created his own filmmaking family.

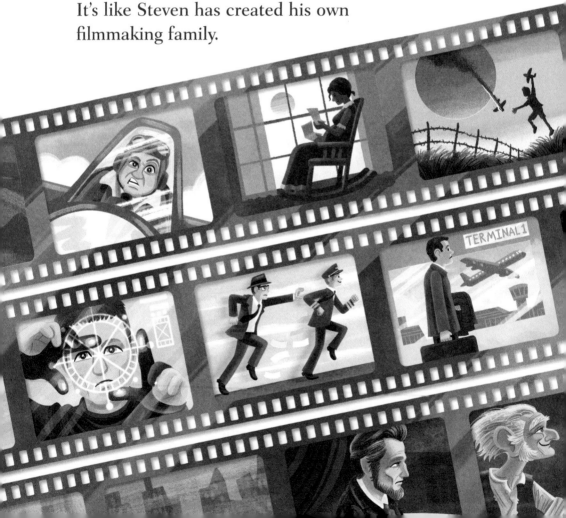

At home, Steven has another family—he's the father of seven children! He has said that directing the young actors in *E.T.* helped him realize he was ready to raise kids of his own.

Steven Spielberg is one of the world's most popular filmmakers. He continues to bring his amazing stories to life with the help of his friends—just as he did when he was a quiet young boy using the family movie camera.

To this day he says, "When I grow up, I still want to be a director."